AF346101

Why Do Birds Sing.

Why Do Birds Sing

Collection

Nature and Human Studies

ISBN : 978-2-38469-031-2
EAN : 9782384690312

Why Birds Sing[1]

I have long been an interested observer of bird-life. The situation of my house and garden, on the terrace-slopes of the Spielberg, affords me favorable opportunities for studying the habits of the feathered tribes. They build their nests in my garden, and lend themselves with great docility to the purposes of the friendly spectator of their movements. At one time the nest of a hedge-sparrow (*Sylvia curruca*) attracted my attention; I noticed particularly the increased care that was taken by the parent birds, as feeding-time approached, against unwelcome discovery. It was manifested, first, in a cessation of singing, and then in the combined efforts of the pair to divert strange looks from the nest. The birds, when about to take food to their young, were

---

[1] By B. Placzek.

accustomed to fly down from opposite sides, and while one, after many cross-flights through the overhanging foliage, slipped into the nest, the other would flutter wildly hither and thither in another part of the tree. The three half-fledged young birds, when able to glide through the bushes, but not yet to fly, were dislodged from the nest, and while two of them disappeared with the mother, I caught the third, against the anxious remonstrances of the male, and hung it up in a cage in my veranda. The old male stood faithful to his chick, evidently concentrating his whole attention upon it, hopping around among the trees and collecting insects for it from early in the morning till the coming on of night, unceasingly, and never out of the neighborhood. He was accustomed to sound a grating *zapp, zapp,* in which the young one soon learned to join, in a variety of tones constituting a whole gamut of modulated sounds, from the note of cheerful pleasure to those of anxiety and anger, and was moved to utterance by the most insignificant event in the cage or around it.

I observed that the male bird, which had sung much less than usual while the female was sitting, and had ceased to sing entirely as soon as the young ones were hatched out, resumed his old habit of song as soon as the fledgeling's domicile was changed from the nest to the cage. He would execute a kind of strophe of from seven to nine clear, ringing notes, having sometimes a joyous and sometimes a melancholy expression. What was the meaning of the song which he thus resumed? Was it poured out to dispel the sorrow of the lonely orphaned young one? Did the absence of the female give the male a greater liberty in the matter? Or, was it sung in hopes of bringing the female back, or in rivalry with another male? Pondering over such questions as these led me to reflections and observations on the origin and meaning of the songs of birds.

While we may regard the ordinary vocal utterances of birds as expressions of their moods and wants, signals of intelligence, notes of warning, or calls for help, their song proper must be supposed to describe their more deep-felt emotions and anxieties, and to be related to their common expressions of sound as art is related to the handicrafts that minister to the necessities of life. Like art, the birdsong also, repeatedly exercised, may become an habitual mode of expression.

The majority of ornithologists agree in ascribing an erotic character to the songs of birds; not only the melting melodies, but also those of their tones that are discordant to the human ear, are regarded as love-notes. Darwin finally, saving some reserves, came to accept this view. To be able to speak critically of the love-song, one should pay especial regard to the love-life of birds. It would be to throw water into the sea to add to what ornithological writers have advanced concerning the exceeding vital worth and cosmical significance of love. Nevertheless, I venture the opinion that the origin of the song-habit is to be found in other sources as well as in this important factor, among which is the joy of life, manifested in an irresistible determination to announce itself in melody; and that the song is more perfectly brought out in proportion as this feeling is more highly developed in the organization.

Birds in freedom begin to sing long before pairing, and continue it, subject to interruptions, long afterward, though all passion has been extinguished; and domesticated birds sing through the whole year without regard to breeding-time, though no female or companion ever be in sight. Such birds, born in captivity, never feel the loss of freedom, and, if they are well taken care of, are always hearty and in good spirits. The bird sings, to a large extent, for his own pleasure; for he frequently lets himself out lustily when he knows he is all alone. In the spring-time of love, when all life is invigorated, and the effort to win a mate by ardent wooing is crowned with the joy of triumph, the song reaches its highest perfection. But the male bird also sings to entertain his mate during the arduous nest-building and hatching, to cheer the young, and, if he be a domesticated bird, to give pleasure to his lord and the providence that takes care of him, and in doing so to please himself. Lastly, the bird sings—by habit, as we call it—because the tendency is innate in the organs of song to exercise themselves.

My male hedge-sparrow, whose truly devoted care of its solitary young one I have described, began, after a ten days' pause, to sing more frequently and intensively, although neither a female nor a male of his species was in the neighborhood, apparently to cheer his ward. His evening farewells, uttered in a clear voice, were peculiarly expressive and touching. When, after eight days more, the chick began of itself to pick food from the dish and to snap at flies, the old bird discontinued its daytime feeding and singing, and came only at night. When the young bird was ready to fly, it came no more.

Female birds, as a rule, do not sing. The mechanism of their vocal apparatus is the same as that of the males, though with a weaker muscularity; and they are not wanting in ability to give melodious and vigorous expression to the exuberance of their life, but they seem to have lost the habit, or to be without the disposition to do so. Some authors, with Daines Barrington and Darwin, regard their non-inclination to sing as a mark of prudence; for it would be dangerous for them to make themselves conspicuous during the breeding-season, and direct the attention of enemies to their nests with their precious contents. But some other authors suggest, and I am inclined to agree with them, that they are restrained by a feminine reserve. The knowledge that the ardor of the male can be stimulated by indifference and inflamed to fury by resistance, prompts the female to practice all the arts of coquetry, of which Mantegazza says: "No woman can surpass the wonderful refinement with which a female canary-bird will offer a seeming of opposition to the passion of the male. All the numerous arts with which the world of women can conceal a 'yes' under a 'no' are as nothing compared with the arrant coquetry, the dissembled efforts to escape, the snappings and bitings, and the thousand tricks of the females of animals." Brehm says that the male finds in the female those desirable and attractive qualities that are wanting in himself. He seeks the opposite to himself with the force of a chemical element.

A loud singing by the female would be as unpleasant to him as a beard on the face of a woman would be to a man. According to an Eastern proverb, man makes love with his speech, woman by her attitude and bearing. Among the feathered races, whose love-life is more largely and intensively developed than that of any other of the families of animals, the female perceives, feels, and knows that a discreet graciousness, a quiet power, and unobtrusive yet expressive, tender, and gentle manifestations, are attractions that operate irresistibly upon the male, and she therefore adopts them in her demeanor toward her suitor. Toussenel remarks: "Song is also given to the female; and, if she makes no use of the faculty, it is because she knows how to do more and better than to sing. She, as well as her brother, has gone through a course of music in her youth, and has cultivated her taste with the years. This cultivation, in fact, filled a need of both birds, for through it the female has become qualified to appreciate the charm of the elegies that are to be sighed out to her, and to award to the most worthy minstrel the prize for his song. The females know well enough how to express themselves in the language of passion when fancy inspires them to it or solitude condemns them to it." Fischer says that female birds begin at the same time with the males to twitter in the first practice of song, although they never pass beyond the stage of blundering at it. Bechstein remarks that the females of the canary bird, bull-finch, robin, and lark utter a melodious song, particularly in widowhood.

Darwin suggests that in some of these cases of female songsters the habit of singing may be ascribed to the fact that the birds are so well cared for and are captive; for such conditions are most likely to disturb all the functions connected with reproduction. Numerous examples have been mentioned of the partial transmission of secondary characteristics of the male to the female; and it is not, therefore, very surprising to find that the females of a few species also possess a fully developed and active faculty of singing. I will only add to these facts that even for a repressed exercise, and with a restricted muscular activity, a force and a proper organ are requisite, and that therefore the gently modulated, muffled sounds, the peeping, whispering, clucking, smacking, and cooing, with which the females respond to the persuasions of the male, control their young, and otherwise express themselves, require a vocal apparatus similar to that of the male, which shall not be stunted by non-use. Instead of regarding, as Darwin did, the singing organs of female birds as an instance of the partial but useless transmission of secondary male characteristics to the female, I think we might now plausibly consider it a transmission in undiminished perfection of a faculty generally characteristic of both, but which is most freely exercised in the male on account of its relation to the most important act of his life, and hence to the maintenance of the species.

Singing out of rivalry finds an explanation in the disposition of the exultant songster to show himself off and to surpass others. If this exultant feeling is wanting, as, for instance, when it is depressed by some uncomfortable condition, the emulative singing stops. Hence, freshly-caught birds are songless in the cage, as are also males when several of them are confined together. In these cases the birds are pining for their lost freedom, or are suffering from the feeling of being crowded or hampered in their movements.

Domesticated birds sing also from a kind of gratitude to please their master, after they have discovered that he likes their songs, and the act produces in return a wholesome effect upon them. Under such influences, they sing all through the year, and more than they would do in freedom. I have had the opportunity of making a remarkable observation which shows that singing-birds desire the notice and applause of their attendant, and are affected by them. I had a yellow thrush (*Turdus saxatilis*), taken from the nest, which had become quite tame and confiding. Its cage hung behind the window-curtain of my study, and this adjoined my bedroom. I sometimes heard early in the morning a clear, melodious cock-crowing that seemed to come from a distant barn-yard. I thought of everything to which I might attribute it except my bird, which had never indulged in anything but the simplest song when I was present; but I soon found out his trick. Having risen early one morning and gone into the study while the bird's head was still hidden under his wing, I sat still in a farther corner of the room till matters began to get lively in the cage. Unobserved by my pet, I could see him through the folds of the curtain stretch out his wings and one foot, and plume himself. Then he found his voice and sounded out the cock-crow which I had heard so often from my bedroom without suspecting its real origin. Had I not seen the bird's mouth open and his throat vibrating, I should still have thought the sound came from a distance. Suddenly I stepped behind the curtain, when the bird, perceiving me, broke off at once in the midst of his crowing—a thing he had never done when I appeared as a witness to his ordinary singing—and fluttered timorously around as if he had done something wrong. I went out from the room and waited near, but the bird did not crow any more, nor again for two days afterward. Then he ventured upon a repetition of his exercise before anything had moved in his neighborhood. I opened the door in the midst of his practice and he stopped, and he never would crow when any one was present. There is nothing particularly remarkable in the crowing of itself, for many birds imitate the sounds made by other animals. The curious fact about this circumstance was, that the bird would not crow in my presence, and would always stop when any one appeared to witness his exercise. There is no evidence that he had ever had an unpleasant experience in connection with crowing. His conduct must therefore be attributed to a kind of feeling of shame, or to a sense of the unfitness of that method of expression to a bird of his character and standing. Have we not in this another proof of the possession by animals of a psychical quality which it has been usual to regard as peculiarly and distinctively human?

The Song of Birds[2].

Birds sing when they are happy, and cry out when they are frightened, just as children do. Only they have songs and cries of their own. You can always tell when the little song-birds are happy, for each one trills out his joyous notes as he sits on a branch of a tree, or the top of a hedge.

In the early morning of the spring, you will hear singing in the garden almost before it is light. First there is a little chirping and twittering, as if the birds were saying "good-morning" and preparing their throats. Then, as the sun rises, there comes a burst of song.

Robins, Thrushes, Blackbirds, Chaffinches, and Wrens whistle away merrily, and many other little birds join in. While they are all singing together, it is not easy to tell one song

---

[2] Arabella Buckley, in Birds of the Air.

from another, though the Thrush sings loudest and clearest of all.

Then they fly away to their breakfast and, as the day goes on, you hear one or two at a time. So you can listen to the notes of each song, and if you go near very quietly, you can see the throat of the bird swelling and quivering as he works the little voice-chords inside, which make the notes.

It is not easy to write down what a bird sings, for it is like whistling—there are no words in it. But people often try to imitate their songs in words. Listen to the Thrush. You can fancy he says "cherry-tree, cherry-tree, cherry-tree" three times. Then, after some other notes, he sings "hurry-up, hurry-up," and "go-it, go-it." For the thrush has a great many notes.

The pretty Yellowhammer, with its bright yellow head, sings "a little bit of bread, and no che-e-s-e." The Chiff-chaff calls "chiff-chaff, chiff-chaff" quite distinctly. Any child can imitate the cuckoo, or the coo-oo-oo of the wood-pigeon.

As the days grow hotter, the birds sing less. They sit on the branches of the trees, or on the hedges under the shade of the leaves, or hop about in the wood.

Then when the evening comes, and long shadows creep over the grass, each bird looks out for his supper. When he is satisfied he sings his evening song of content, before he goes to sleep.

What a concert it is! Finches, tomtits, sparrows, wrens, robins, and chaffinches all singing at once. And above them all, come the song of the thrushes and blackbirds, the cooing of the wood-pigeon and the caw-caw of the rooks as they fly home from the fields. As the thrushes were the first to begin in the morning, except the lark, so they are the last to leave off at night, and often one thrush will go on long after all the others are quiet.

Then at last all seem to have settled down for the night. But no! If you live in Kent, or any part of the south or east of England, you may hear in May or June a sweet sound, like a flute, coming softly from many parts of the wood. This comes from the Nightingales, who, in the warm summer, will sing nearly all night.

They sing in the day as well, but their note is so soft that often you cannot hear it when more noisy birds are singing. In the still night you can hear the sweet song rising up six notes and then bubbling like a flute played in water. When you have once heard a nightingale sing you will never forget it. In Yorkshire or Devonshire you will not hear him, for he does not go so far to the North or to the West.

Birds sing most in the spring, for then they are making their nests, and the father bird sings to the mother while she is building, and when she is sitting on the eggs. You may often find out where a Robin's nest is hidden by seeing the cock-robin sitting on a branch singing to his mate. Most people too, have seen the Wood-pigeon puffing out his throat and cooing and bowing to the mother bird on her nest. For pigeons make love all the year round.

When the mother bird is sitting, the father bird sings for joy, and when the young birds are hatched he teaches them his song. Song-birds have very delicate throats. They have muscles, which quiver like the strings of a violin, and the young birds have to learn to work these muscles.

It is curious to hear a young Blackbird or Thrush beginning to try a tune. First he sounds one note, then two or three. They are not always in tune, but he tries again and again. So little by little he learns his father's song.

Bird Songs[3].

Why do birds sing? Has their music a meaning, or is it all a matter of blind impulse? Some bright morning in March, as you go out-of-doors, you are greeted by the notes of the first robin. Perched in a leafless tree, there he sits, facing the sun like a genuine fire-worshiper, and singing as though he would pour out his very soul. What is he thinking about? What spirit possesses him?

It is easy to ask questions until the simplest matter comes to seem, what at bottom it really is, a thing altogether mysterious; but if our robin could understand us, he would, likely enough, reply:—

"Why do you talk in this way, as if it were something requiring explanation that a bird

---

[3] By Bradford Torrey, *Birds in the Bush*.

should sing? You seem to have forgotten that everybody sings, or almost everybody. Think of the insects,—the bees and the crickets and the locusts, to say nothing of your intimate friends, the mosquitoes! Think, too, of the frogs and the hylas! If these cold-blooded, low-lived creatures, after sleeping all winter in the mud, are free to make so much use of their voices, surely a bird of the air may sing his unobtrusive song without being cross-examined concerning the purpose of it. Why do the mice sing, and the monkeys, and the woodchucks? Indeed, sir,—if one may be so bold,—why do you sing, yourself?"

This matter-of-fact Darwinism need not frighten us. It will do us no harm to remember, now and then, "the hole of the pit whence we were digged;" and besides, as far as any relationship between us and the birds is concerned, it is doubtful whether we are the party to complain.

But avoiding "genealogies and contentions," and taking up the question with which we began, we may safely say that birds sing, sometimes to gratify an innate love for sweet sounds; sometimes to win a mate, or to tell their love to a mate already won; sometimes as practice, with a view to self-improvement; and sometimes for no better reason than the poet's,—"I do but sing because I must." In general, they sing for joy; and their joy, of course, has various causes.

For one thing, they are very sensitive to the weather. With them, as with us, sunlight and a genial warmth go to produce serenity. A bright summer-like day, late in October, or even in November, will set the smaller birds to singing, and the grouse to drumming. I heard a robin venturing a little song on the 25th of last December; but that, for aught I know, was a Christmas carol. No matter what the season, you will not hear a great deal of bird music during a high wind; and if you are caught in the woods by a sudden shower in May or June, and are not too much taken up with thoughts of your own condition, you will hardly fail to notice the instant silence which falls upon the woods with the rain. Birds, however, are more or less inconsistent (that is, a part of their likeness to us), and sometimes sing most freely when the sky is overcast.

But their highest joys are by no means dependent upon the moods of the weather. A comfortable state of mind is not to be contemned, but beings who are capable of deep and passionate affection recognize a difference between comfort and ecstasy. And the peculiar glory of birds is just here, in the all-consuming fervor of their love. It would be commonplace to call them models of conjugal and parental faithfulness. With a few exceptions (and these, it is a pleasure to add, not singers), the very least of them is literally faithful unto death. Here and there, in the notes of some collector, we are told of a difficulty he has had in securing a coveted specimen: the tiny creature, whose mate had been already "collected," would persist in hovering so closely about the invader's head that it was impossible to shoot him without spoiling him for the cabinet by blowing him to pieces!

Need there be any mystery about the singing of such a lover? Is it surprising if at times he is so enraptured that he can no longer sit tamely on the branch, but must dart into the air, and go circling round and round, caroling as he flies?

So far as song is the voice of emotion, it will of necessity vary with the emotion; and everyone who has ears must have heard once in a while bird music of quite unusual fervor. For example, I have often seen the least flycatcher (a very unromantic-looking body, surely) when he was almost beside himself; flying in a circle, and repeating breathlessly his emphatic *chebec*. And once I found a wood pewee in a somewhat similar mood. He was more quiet than the least flycatcher; but he too sang on the wing, and I have never heard notes which seemed more expressive of happiness. Many of them were entirely new and strange, although the familiar *pewee* was introduced among the rest. As I listened, I felt it to be an occasion for thankfulness that the delighted creature had never studied anatomy, and did not know that the structure of his throat made it improper for him to sing. In this connection, also, I recall a cardinal grosbeak, whom I heard several years ago, on the bank of the Potomac River. An old soldier had taken me to visit the Great Falls, and as we were clambering over the rocks this grosbeak began to sing; and soon, without any hint from me, and without knowing who the invisible musician was, my companion remarked upon the uncommon beauty of the song. The cardinal is always a great singer, having a voice which, as European writers say, is almost equal to the nightingale's; but in this case the more stirring, martial quality of the strain had given place to an exquisite mellowness, as if it were, what I have no doubt it was, a song of love.

Every kind of bird has notes of its own, so that a thoroughly practiced ear would be able to discriminate the different species with nearly as much certainty as Professor Baird would feel after an examination of the anatomy and plumage. Still this strong specific resemblance is far from being a dead uniformity. Aside from the fact, already mentioned, that the characteristic strain is sometimes given with extraordinary sweetness and emphasis, there are often to be detected variations of a more formal character. This is noticeably true of robins. It may almost be said that no two of them sing alike; while now and then their vagaries are conspicuous enough to attract general attention. One who was my neighbor last year interjected into his song a series of four or five most exact imitations of the peep of a chicken. When I first heard this performance, I was in company with two friends, both of whom noticed and laughed at it; and some days afterwards I visited the spot again, and found the bird still rehearsing the same ridiculous medley. I conjectured that he had been brought up near a hen-coop, and, moreover, had been so unfortunate as to lose his father before his notes had become thoroughly fixed; and then, being compelled to finish his musical education by himself, had taken a fancy to practice these chicken calls. This guess may not have been correct. All I can affirm is that he sang exactly as he might have been expected to do, on that supposition; but certainly the resemblance seemed too close to be accidental.

The variations of the wood thrush are fully as striking as those of the robin, and sometimes it is impossible not to feel that the artist is making a deliberate effort to do something out of the ordinary course, something better than he has ever done before. Now and then he prefaces his proper song with many disconnected, extremely *staccato* notes, following each other at very distant and unexpected intervals of pitch. It is this, I conclude, which is meant by some writer (who it is I cannot now remember) when he criticises the wood thrush for spending too much time in tuning his instrument. But the fault is the critic's, I think; to my ear these preliminaries sound rather like the recitative which goes before the grand *aria*.

Still another musician who delights to take liberties with his score is the towhee bunting, or chewink. Indeed, he carries the matter so far that sometimes it seems almost as if he suspected the proximity of some self-conceited ornithologist, and were determined, if possible, to make a fool of him. And for my part, being neither self conceited nor an ornithologist, I am willing to confess that I have once or twice been so badly deceived that now the mere sight of this *Pipilo* is, so to speak, a means of grace to me.

One more of these innovators (these heretics, as they are most likely called by their more conservative brethren) is the field sparrow, better known as *Spizella pusilla*. His usual song consists of a simple line of notes, beginning leisurely, but growing shorter and more rapid to the close. The voice is so smooth and sweet, and the acceleration so well managed, that, although the whole is commonly a strict monotone, the effect is not in the least monotonous. This song I once heard rendered in reverse order, with a result so strange that I did not suspect the identity of the author till I had crept up within sight of him. Another of these sparrows, who has passed the last two seasons in my neighborhood, habitually doubles the measure; going through it in the usual way, and then, just as you expect him to conclude, catching it up again, *Da capo*.

But birds like these are quite outdone by such species as the song sparrow, the white-eyed vireo, and the Western meadow-lark,— species of which we may say that each individual bird has a whole repertory of songs at his command. The song sparrow, who is the best known of the three, will repeat one melody perhaps a dozen times, then change it for a second, and in turn leave that for a third; as if he were singing hymns of twelve or fifteen stanzas each, and set each hymn to its appropriate tune. It is something well worth listening to, common though it is, and may easily suggest a number of questions about the origin and meaning of bird music.

The white-eyed vireo is a singer of astonishing spirit, and his sudden changes from one theme to another are sometimes almost startling. He is a skillful ventriloquist, also, and I remember one in particular who outwitted me completely. He was rehearsing a well-known strain, but at the end there came up from the bushes underneath a querulous call. At first I took it for granted that some other bird was in the underbrush; but the note was repeated too many times, and came in too exactly on the beat.

I have no personal acquaintance with the Western meadow-lark, but no less than twenty-six of his songs have been printed in musical notation, and these are said to be by no means all.

Others of our birds have similar gifts, though no others, so far as I know, are quite so versatile as these three. Several of the warblers, for example, have attained to more than one set song, notwithstanding the deservedly small reputation of this misnamed family. I have myself heard the golden-crowned thrush, the black-throated green warbler, the black-throated blue, the yellow-rumped, and the chestnut-sided, sing two melodies each, while the blue golden-winged has at least three; and this, of course, without making anything of slight variations such as all birds are more or less accustomed to indulge in. The best of the three songs of the blue golden-wing I have never heard except on one occasion, but then it was repeated for half an hour under my very eyes. It bore no resemblance to the common *dsee, dsee, dsee,* of the species, and would appear to be seldom used; for not only have I never heard it since, but none of the writers seem ever to have heard it at all. However, I still keep a careful description of it, which I took down on the spot, and which I expect some future golden-wing to verify.

But the most celebrated of the warblers in this regard is the golden-crowned thrush, otherwise called the oven-bird and the wood wagtail. His ordinary effort is one of the noisiest, least melodious, and most incessant sounds to be heard in our woods. His *song* is another matter. For that he takes to the air (usually starting from a tree-top, although I have seen him rise from the ground), whence, after a preliminary *chip, chip,* he lets fall a hurried flood of notes, in the midst of which can usually be distinguished his familiar *weechee, weechee, weechee.* It is nothing wonderful that he should sing on the wing,—

many other birds do the same, and very much better than he; but he is singular in that he strictly reserves his aerial music for late in the afternoon. I have heard it as early as three o'clock, but never before that, and it is most common about sunset. Writers speak of it as limited to the season of courtship; but I have heard it almost daily till near the end of July, and once, for my special benefit, perhaps, it was given in full—and repeated—on the first day of September. But who taught the little creature to do this,—to sing one song in the forenoon, perched upon a twig, and to keep another for afternoon, singing that invariably on the wing? and what difference is there between the two in the mind of the singer?

It is an indiscretion ever to say of a bird that he has only such and such notes. You may have been his friend for years, but the next time you go into the woods he will likely enough put you to shame by singing something not so much as hinted at in your description. I thought I knew the song of the yellow-rumped warbler, having listened to it many times,—a slight and rather characterless thing, nowise remarkable. But coming down Mount Willard one day in June, I heard a warbler's song which brought me to a sudden halt. It was new and beautiful,—more beautiful, it seemed at the moment, than any warbler's song I had ever heard. What could it be? A little patient waiting (while the black-flies and mosquitoes "came upon me to eat up my flesh"), and the wonderful stranger appeared in full view,—my old acquaintance, the yellow-rumped warbler.

With all this strong tendency on the part of birds to vary their music, how is it that there is still such a degree of uniformity, so that, as we have said, every species may be recognized by its notes? Why does every red-eyed vireo sing in one way, and every white-eyed vireo in another? Who teaches the young chipper to trill, and the young linnet to warble? In short, how do birds come by their music? Is it all a matter of instinct, inherited habit, or do they learn it? The answer appears to be that birds sing as children talk, by simple imitation. Nobody imagines that the infant is born with a language printed upon his brain. The father and mother may never have known a word of any tongue except the English, but if the child is brought up to hear only Chinese, he will infallibly speak that, and nothing else. And careful experiments have shown the same to be true of birds. Taken from the nest just after they leave the shell, they invariably sing, not their own so-called natural song, but the song of their foster-parents; provided, of course, that this is not anything beyond their physical capacity. The notorious house sparrow (our "English" sparrow), in his wild or semi-domesticated state, never makes a musical sound; but if he is taken in hand early enough, he may be taught to sing, so it is said, nearly as well as the canary. Bechstein relates that a Paris clergyman had two of these sparrows whom he had trained to speak, and, among other things, to recite several of the shorter commandments; and the narrative goes on to say that it was sometimes very comical, when the pair were disputing over their food, to hear one gravely admonish the other, "Thou shalt not steal!" It would be interesting to know why creatures thus gifted do not sing of their own motion. With their amiability and sweet peaceableness they ought to be caroling the whole year round.

This question of the transmission of songs from one generation to another is, of course, a part of the general subject of animal intelligence, a subject much discussed in these days on account of its bearing upon the modern doctrine concerning the relation of man to the inferior orders.

We have nothing to do with such a theme, but it may not be out of place to suggest to preachers and moralists that here is a striking and unhackneyed illustration of the force of early training. Birds sing by imitation, it is true, but as a rule they imitate only the notes which they hear during the first few weeks after they are hatched. One of Mr. Barrington's linnets, for example, after being educated under a titlark, was put into a room with two birds of his own species, where he heard them sing freely every day for three months. He made no attempt to learn anything from them, however, but kept on practicing what the titlark had taught him, quite unconscious of anything singular or unpatriotic in such a course. This law, that impressions received during the immaturity of the powers become the unalterable habit of the after life, is perhaps the most momentous of all the laws in whose power we find ourselves. Sometimes we are tempted to call it cruel. But if it were annulled, this would be a strange world. What a hurly-hurly we should have among the birds! There would be no more telling them by their notes. Thrushes and jays, wrens and chickadees, finches and warblers, all would be singing one grand medley.

Between these two opposing tendencies, one urging to variation, the other to permanence (for Nature herself is half radical, half conservative), the language of birds has grown from rude beginnings to its present beautiful diversity; and whoever lives a century of millenniums hence will listen to music such as we in this day can only dream of. Inappreciably but ceaselessly the work goes on. Here and there is born a master-singer, a feathered genius, and every generation makes its own addition to the glorious inheritance.

It may be doubted whether there is any real connection between moral character and the possession of wings. Nevertheless there has long been a popular feeling that some such congruity does exist; and certainly it seems unreasonable to suppose that creatures who are able to soar at will into the heavens should be without other equally angelic attributes. But, be that as it may, our friends, the birds, do undeniably set us a good example in several respects. To mention only one, how becoming is their observance of morning and evening song! In spite of their industrious spirit (and few of us labor more hours daily), neither their first nor their last thoughts are given to the question, What shall we eat, and what shall we drink? Possibly their habit of saluting the rising and setting sun may be thought to favor the theory that the worship of the god of day was the original religion. I know nothing about that. But it would be a sad change if the birds, declining from their present beautiful custom, were to sleep and work, work and sleep, with no holy hour between, as is too much the case with the being who, according to his own pharisaic notion, is the only religious animal.

In the season, however, the woods are by no means silent, even at noonday. Many species (such as the vireos and warblers, who get their living amid the foliage of trees) sing as they work; while the thrushes and others, who keep business and pleasure more distinct, are often too happy to go many hours together without a hymn. I have even seen robins singing without quitting the turf; but that is rather unusual, for somehow birds have come to feel that they must get away from the ground when the lyrical mood is upon them. This may be a thing of sentiment (for is not language full of uncomplimentary allusions to earth and earthliness?), but more likely it is prudential. The gift of song is no doubt a dangerous blessing to creatures who have so many enemies, and we can readily believe that they have found it safer to be up where they can look about them while thus publishing their whereabouts.

A very interesting exception to this rule is the savanna sparrow, who sings habitually from the ground. But even he shares the common feeling, and stretches himself to his full height with an earnestness which is almost laughable, in view of the result; for his notes are hardly louder than a cricket's chirp. Probably he has fallen into this lowly habit from living in meadows and salt marshes, where bushes and trees are not readily to be come at; and it is worth noticing that, in the case of the skylark and the white-winged blackbird, the same conditions have led to a result precisely opposite. The sparrow, we may presume, was originally of a humble disposition, and when nothing better offered itself for a singing-perch easily grew accustomed to standing upon a stone or a little lump of earth; and this practice, long persisted in, naturally had the effect to lessen the loudness of his voice. The skylark, on the other hand, when he did not readily find a tree-top, said to himself, "Never mind! I have a pair of wings." And so the lark is famous, while the sparrow remains unheard-of, and is even mistaken for a grasshopper.

How true it is that the very things which dishearten one nature and break it down, only help another to find out what it was made for! If you would foretell the development, either of a bird or of a man, it is not enough to know his environment, you must know also what there is in him.

We have possibly made too much of the savanna sparrow's innocent eccentricity. He fills his place, and fills it well; and who knows but that he may yet outshine the skylark? There is a promise, I believe, for those who humble themselves. But what shall be said of species which do not even try to sing, and that, notwithstanding they have all the structural peculiarities of singing birds, and must, almost certainly, have come from ancestors who were singers? We have already mentioned the house sparrow, whose defect is the more mysterious on account of his belonging to so highly musical a family. But *he* was never accused of not being noisy enough, while we have one bird who, though he is classed with the oscines, passes his life in almost unbroken silence. Of course I refer to the waxwing, or cedar-bird, whose faint, sibilant whisper can scarcely be thought to contradict the foregoing description. By what strange freak he has lapsed into this ghostly habit, nobody knows. I make no account of the insinuation that he gave up music because it hindered his success in cherry-stealing. He likes cherries, it is true; and who can blame him? But he would need to work hard to steal more than does that indefatigable songster, the robin. I feel sure he has some better reason than this for his Quakerish conduct. But, however he came by his stillness, it is likely that by this time he plumes himself upon it. Silence is golden, he thinks, the supreme result of the highest æsthetic culture. Those loud creatures, the thrushes and finches! What a vulgar set they are, to be sure, the more's the pity! Certainly if he does not reason in some such way, bird nature is not so human as we have given it credit for being. Besides, the waxwing has an uncommon appreciation of the decorous; at least, we must think so if we are able to credit a story of Nuttall's. He declares that a Boston gentleman, whose name he gives, saw one of a company of these birds capture an insect, and offer it to his neighbor; he, however, delicately declined the dainty bit, and it was offered to the next, who, in turn, was equally polite; and the morsel actually passed back and forth along the line, till, finally, one of the flock was persuaded to eat it. I have never seen anything equal to this; but one day, happening to stop under a low cedar, I discovered right over my head a waxwing's nest with the mother-bird sitting upon it, while her mate was perched beside her on the branch. He was barely out of my reach, but he did not move a muscle; and although he uttered no sound, his behavior said as plainly as possible, "What do you expect to do *here*? Don't you see *I* am standing guard over this nest?" I should be ashamed not to be able to add that I respected his dignity and courage, and left him and his castle unmolested.

Observations so discursive as these can hardly be finished; they must break off abruptly, or else go on forever. Let us make an end, therefore, with expressing our hope that the cedar-bird, already so handsome and chivalrous, will yet take to himself a song; one sweet and original, worthy to go with his soft satin coat, his ornaments of sealing-wax, and his magnificent top-knot. Let him do that, and he shall always be made welcome; yes, even though he come in force and in cherry-time.

The Singing-Birds and their Songs[4]

Those persons enjoy the most happiness, if possessed of a benevolent heart and favored by ordinary circumstances of fortune, who have acquired by habit and education the power of deriving pleasure from objects that lie immediately around them. But these common sources of happiness are opened to those only who are endowed with genius, or who have received a certain kind of intellectual training. The more ordinary the mental and moral organization and culture of the individual, the more far-fetched and dear-bought must be his enjoyments. Nature has given us in full development only those appetites which are necessary to our physical well-being. She has left our moral appetites

---

[4] In A.M., vol.2 ; 1858.

and capacities in the germ, to be developed by education and circumstances. Hence those agreeable sensations that come chiefly from the exercise of the imagination, which may be called the pleasures of sentiment, are available only to persons of a peculiar refinement of mind. The ignorant and rude may be dazzled and delighted by physical beauty, and charmed by loud and stirring sounds; but those more simple melodies and less attractive colors and forms that appeal to the mind for their principal effect act more powerfully upon individuals of superior culture.

In proportion as we have been trained to be agreeably affected by the outward forms of Nature, and the sounds that proceed from the animate and inanimate world, are we capable of being made happy without resorting to expensive and vulgar recreations. It ought, therefore, to be one of the chief points in the education of youth, while teaching them the still more important offices of humanity, to cultivate and enliven their susceptibility to the charms of natural objects. Then would the aspects of Nature, continually changing with the progress of the seasons and the sounds that enliven their march, satisfy, in a great measure, that craving for agreeable sensations which leads mankind away from humble and healthful pursuits to those of a more artificial and exciting life. The value of such pleasures consists not so much in their cheapness as in their favorable moral influences, which improve the heart, while they lead the mind to observations that pleasantly exercise and develop, without tasking its powers. The quiet emotions, half musical and half poetical, which are awakened by listening to the songs of birds, belong to this class of refined enjoyments.

But the music of birds, though agreeable to all, conveys positive and durable pleasure only to those who have learned to associate with their notes, in connection with the scenes of Nature, a thousand interesting and romantic images. To many persons of this character it affords more delight than the most brilliant music of the opera or the concert. In vain, therefore, will it be said, as an objection, that the notes of birds have no charm, save that which is derived from association, and that, considered as music, they do not equal that of the most simple reed or flageolet. It is sufficient to remark, that the most delightful influences of Nature proceed from those sights and sounds that appeal to the imagination and affections through the medium of slight and almost insensible impressions made upon the eye and the ear. At the moment when these physical impressions exceed a certain mean, the spell is broken, and the enjoyment becomes sensual, not intellectual. How soon, indeed, would the songs of birds lose their effect, if they were loud and brilliant, like a band of instruments! It is their simplicity that gives them their charm.

As a further illustration of this point, it may be remarked that simple melodies have among all people exercised a greater power over the imagination than louder and more complicated music. Nature employs a very small amount of physical sensation to create an intellectual passion, and when an excess is used a diminished effect is produced. I am persuaded that the effect of a great part of our sacred music is lost by an excess of harmony and a too great volume of sound. On the same principle, a loud crash of thunder deafens and terrifies; but its low and distant rumbling produces an agreeable emotion of sublimity.

The songs of birds are as intimately allied with poetry as with music. The lark has been aptly denominated a "feathered lyric" by one of the English poets; and the analogy becomes apparent when we consider how much the song of a bird resembles a lyrical ballad in its influence on the mind. Though it utters no words, how plainly it suggests a long train of agreeable images of love, beauty, friendship, and home! When a young person has suffered any severe wound of the affections, he seldom fails, if endowed with a sensitive mind, to listen to the birds as sharers in his affliction. Through them the deities of the groves seem to offer him their consolation. By indulging this habit of making companionship with the objects of Nature, all pleasing sights and sounds gradually become certain anodynes for his sorrow; and those who have this mental alembic for turning grief into a poetic melancholy can seldom be reduced to a state of absolute despondency. Poetry, or rather the poetic sentiment, exalts all our pleasures and soothes all our afflictions by some illusive charm, whether it be turned into the channel of religion or romance. Without this reflection of light from the imagination, what is the passion of love? and what is our love of beauty and of sweet sounds, but a mere gravitation?

The voice of every singing-bird has its associations in the minds of all susceptible persons who were born and nurtured within the precincts of its untutored minstrelsy. The music of birds is modulated in pleasant unison with all the chords of affection and imagination, filling the soul with a lively consciousness of happiness and beauty, and soothing it with romantic visions of memory,- of love, when it was an ethereal sentiment of adoration and not a passion, and of friendship, when it was a passion and not an expedience, - of dear and simple adventures, and of comrades who had part in them, of dappled mornings, and serene and glowing sunsets, - of sequestered nooks and mossy seats in the old wood,--of paths by the riverside, and flowers that smiled a bright welcome to our rambling,--of lingering departures from home, and of old by-ways, overshadowed by trees and hedged with roses and viburnums, that spread their shade and their perfume around our path to gladden our return. By this pleasant instrumentality has Nature provided for the happiness of those who have learned to be delighted with the survey of her works, and with the sound of those voices which she has appointed to communicate to the human soul the joys of her inferior creation.

The singing-birds, with reference to their songs, may be divided into four classes. First, the Rapid Singers, whose song is uninterrupted, of considerable length, and uttered with fervor, and in apparent ecstasy. Second, the Moderate Singers, whose notes are slowly modulated, but without pauses or rests between their different strains. Third, the Interrupted Singers, who seldom modulate their notes with rapidity, and make decided pauses between their several strains, of which there are in general from five to eight or nine. Fourth, the Warblers, whose notes consist of only one or two strains, not combined into a song.

The canary, among foreign birds, and the linnet and bobolink, among American birds, are familiar examples of the first class; the common robin and the veery of the second; the wood-thrush, the cat-bird, and the mocking-bird, of the third; and the blue-bird, the pewee, and the purple martin, of the fourth class. It may be added, that some birds are nearly periodical in their habits of singing, preferring the morning and evening, and occasional periods in other parts of the day, while others sing almost indifferently at all hours. The greater number of species, however, are more tuneful in the early morning than at any other hour.

June, in this part of the world, is the most vocal month of the year. Many of our principal songsters do not arrive until near the middle of May; and all, whether they come early or late, continue in song throughout the month of June. The bobolink, which is one of the first to become silent, continues vocal until the second week in July. So nearly simultaneous is the discontinuance of the songs of this species, that it might seem as if their silence were preconcerted, and that by a vote they had, on a certain day, adjourned over to another year. If an unusually genial day occurs about the seventh of July, we may hear multitudes of them singing merrily on that occasion. Should this time be followed by two or three successive days of chilly and rainy weather, their tunefulness is so generally brought to a close during this period, that we may not hear another musical note from a single individual after the seventh. The songs of birds are discontinued as soon as their amorous dalliances and the care of their offspring have ceased. Hence those birds that raise but one brood of young during the season, like the bobolink, are the first to become silent.

No one of the New England birds is an autumnal warbler; though the song-sparrow often greets the fine mornings in October with his lays, and the shore-lark, after spending the summer in Labrador and about the shores of Hudson's Bay, is sometimes heard in autumn, soaring and singing at the dawn of day, while on his passage to the South. The bobolink, the veery, or Wilson's thrush, the red thrush, and the golden robin, are silent after the middle of July; the wood-thrush, the cat-bird, and the common robin, not until a month later; but the song-sparrow alone continues to sing throughout the summer. The tuneful season of the year, in New England, embraces a period of about four months, from the middle of April to the middle of August.

There are certain times of the day, as well as certain seasons of the year, when the birds are most musical. The grand concert of the feathered tribe takes place during the hour between dawn and sunrise. During the remainder of the day they sing less in concert, though many species are very musical at noonday, and seem, like the nocturnal birds, to prefer the hour when others are silent. At sunset there is an apparent attempt to unite once more in chorus, but this is far from being so loud or so general as in the morning. The little birds which I have classed in the fourth division are a very important accompaniment to the anthem of dawn, their notes, though short, serving agreeably to fill up the pauses made by the other musicians. Thus, the hair-bird (Fringilla Socialis) has a sharp and trilling note, without any modulation, and not at all melodious, when heard alone; but in the morning it is the chief harmonizer of the whole chorus, and serves, more than any other voice, to give unity and symphony to the multitude of miscellaneous parts.

There are not many birds whose notes could be accurately described upon the gamut. The nearest approach we can make to accuracy is to give some general idea of their time and modulation. Their musical intervals can be distinguished but with difficulty, on account of the rapidity of their utterance. I have often attempted to transcribe some of their notes upon the musical scale, but I am persuaded that such sketches can be only approximations to literal correctness. As different individuals of the same species sing very differently, the notes, as transcribed from the song of one individual, will never exactly represent the song of another. If we listen attentively, however, to a number of songs, we shall detect in all of them a theme, as it is termed by musicians, of which the different individuals of the species warble their respective variations. Every song is, technically speaking, a _fantasia_ constructed upon this theme, from which none of the species ever departs.

It is very generally believed that the singing-birds are confined to temperate latitudes, and that the tropical birds have not the gift of song. That this is an error is apparent from the testimony of travellers, who speak of the birds in the Sandwich Islands and New Zealand as singing delightfully, and some fine songsters are occasionally imported in cages from tropical climates. The origin of this notion may be explained in several ways. It is worthy of notice that within the tropics the singing season of different species of birds does not occur at the same time. One species may be musical in the spring, another in summer, and others in autumn and winter.

When one species, therefore, has begun to sing, another has ceased, so that, at whatever time of the year the traveller stops, he hears but few birds engaged in song.

In the temperate latitudes, on the contrary, as soon as the birds arrive, they commence building their nests, and become musical at the same time. If a stranger from a tropical climate should arrive in this country in the spring, and remain here during the months of May and June, he would hear more birds singing together than he ever heard at once in his own clime; but were he to arrive about the middle of July, when the greater number of our birds have discontinued their songs, he would probably, if he knew the reputation of the Northern birds, marvel a little at their silence. If there are as many birds singing at one time during the whole year, in the hot climates, as we hear in this country in the latter half of summer, the greater average would appear to be on the side of the former.

It may also be remarked, that the singing-birds of the tropics are not so well known as those of temperate latitudes which are inhabited by civilized men. The savages and barbarians, who are the principal inhabitants of hot countries, are seldom observant of the habits or the voices of the singing-birds. A musician of the feathered race, as well as a harpist or violinist, must have an appreciating audience, or his powers can never be made known to the world. But even with the same audience, the tropical singing-birds would probably be less esteemed than songsters of equal merit in the temperate latitudes; for, amid the stridulous and deafening sounds made by the insects in warm climates, the notes of birds would be scarcely audible.

We are still inclined to believe, however, that there is a larger proportion of musical birds in the temperate than in the torrid zone, because in the former region there are more of those species that build low and live among the grass and shrubbery, and it is well known that the singing-birds are mostly of the latter description. In warm climates the vegetation consists chiefly of trees and tall vines, forming together an umbrageous canopy overhead, with but a scanty undergrowth. In temperate latitudes the shrubbery predominates, especially in the most northerly parts. Moreover, the grasses that furnish by their seeds a great proportion of the food of the smaller birds are almost entirely wanting in the torrid zone.

The birds that live in trees are remarkable for their brilliant plumage; those that live upon the ground and in the shrubbery are plainly dressed. This is a provision of Nature for their protection, as the ground-birds must have a predominance of tints that resemble the general hues of the surface of the earth. I do not know a single brightly-plumed bird that nestles upon the ground, unless the bobolink may be considered an exception. They are almost invariably colored like sparrows. The birds that inhabit the trees, on the other hand, need less of this protection, though the females are commonly of an olive or greenish yellow, which harmonizes with the general hue of the foliage, and screens them from observation, while sitting upon the nest. The male, on the contrary, who seldom sits upon the nest, requires a plumage that will render him conspicuous to the female and to the young, after they have left their nest. It is remarkable, that Nature, in all cases in which she has created a difference in the plumage of the male and female, has used the hues of their plumage only for the protection of the mother and the young, for whose advantage she has dressed the male parent in colors that must somewhat endanger his own safety.

The color of the plumage of birds seems to bear less relation to their powers of song than to their habitats; and as the birds that live in trees are commonly less tuneful, they are more brilliantly arrayed. The bird employs his song in wooing his mate, as well as in entertaining her after she is wedded; and it is not unlikely that Nature may have compensated those which are deficient in song by giving them a superior beauty of plumage. As the offices of courtship devolve entirely upon the males, it is the more necessary that they should be possessed of conspicuous attractions; but as the task of sitting upon the nest devolves upon the female, she requires more of that protection which arises from the conformity of her plumage with the general hue of the objects that surround her nest. While she is sitting, the plain hues of her dress protect her from observation; but when she leaves her nest to seek her companion, she is enabled by his brilliant colors the more easily to discover him. The male is diligent in providing for the wants of the offspring, and hence it is important that his dress should render him conspicuous. When the young birds have left the nest, upon seeing the flash of his plumage, they immediately utter their call, and by this note, which might not otherwise be sounded at the right moment, he detects them and supplies them with food. Should a bird of prey suddenly come into their neighborhood, he overlooks the plainly-dressed mother and off-spring, and gives chase to the male parent, who not only escapes, but at the same time diverts the attention of the foe from his defenseless progeny.

But the birds that build low, either upon the ground or among the shrubbery, are exposed to a greater number and variety of enemies.

Hence it becomes necessary that the males as well as the females should have that protection which is afforded by sobriety of color. Not being made conspicuous by their plumage, they are endowed with the gift of song, that they may make known their presence to their mate and their young by their voice. I have often thought that the song of the bird was designed by Nature for the benefit of the young, no less than for the entertainment of his mate. The sounds uttered by birds on account of their young always precede the period of incubation. The common hen begins to cluck several days before she begins to sit upon her eggs. In like manner the male singing-bird commences his song when the pair are making ready to build their nest. While his mate is sitting, his song reminds her of his presence, and inspires her with a feeling of security and content, during the period of her confinement. As soon as the young are hatched, they begin to learn his voice and grow accustomed to it, and when they fly from the nest they are prevented by the sound of it from wandering and getting bewildered. If they happen to fly beyond certain bounds, the song of the male parent warns them of their distance, and causes them to turn and draw near the place from which it seems to issue. Thus the song of the male bird, always uttered within a certain circumference, of which the nest is the centre, becomes a kind of sentinel voice, to keep the young birds within prudent limits.

It is not easy to explain why a larger proportion of the birds that occupy trees should be destitute of song, except on the supposition that in such elevated situations the young are more easily guided by sight than by hearing. Still there are many songsters which are dressed in brilliant plumage, and of these we have some examples among our native birds. These, however, are evident exceptions to the general fact, and we may trace a plain analogy in this respect between birds and insects. The musical insects are, we believe, invariably destitute of brilliant plumage. Butterflies and moths do not sing; the music of insects comes chiefly from the plainly-dressed locust and grasshopper tribes.

Bird-Songs[5]

I suspect it requires a special gift of grace to enable one to hear the bird-songs; some new power must be added to the ear, or some obstruction removed. There are not only scales upon our eyes so that we do not see, there are scales upon our ears so that we do not hear. A city woman who had spent much of her time in the country once asked a well-known ornithologist to take her where she could hear the bluebird. "What, never heard the bluebird!" said he. "I have not," said the woman. "Then you will never hear it," said the bird-lover; never hear it with that inward ear that gives beauty and meaning to the note. He could probably have taken her in a few minutes where she could have heard the call or warble of the bluebird; but it would have

---

[5] By John Burroughs, in *Ways of Nature*.

fallen upon unresponsive ears—upon ears that were not sensitized by love for the birds or associations with them. Bird-songs are not music, properly speaking, but only suggestions of music. A great many people whose attention would be quickly arrested by the same volume of sound made by a musical instrument or by artificial means never hear them at all. The sound of a boy's penny whistle there in the grove or the meadow would separate itself more from the background of nature, and be a greater challenge to the ear, than is the strain of the thrush or the song of the sparrow. There is something elusive, indefinite, neutral, about bird-songs that makes them strike obliquely, as it were, upon the ear; and we are very apt to miss them. They are a part of nature, the Nature that lies about us, entirely occupied with her own affairs, and quite regardless of our presence. Hence it is with bird-songs as it is with so many other things in nature—they are what we make them; the ear that hears them must be half creative. I am always disturbed when persons not especially observant of birds ask me to take them where they can hear a particular bird, in whose song they have become interested through a description in some book. As I listen with them, I feel like apologizing for the bird: it has a bad cold, or has just heard some depressing news; it will not let itself out. The song seems so casual and minor when you make a dead set at it. I have taken persons to hear the hermit thrush, and I have fancied that they were all the time saying to themselves, "Is that all?" But should one hear the bird in his walk, when the mind is attuned to simple things and is open and receptive, when expectation is not aroused and the song comes as a surprise out of the dusky silence of the woods, then one feels that it merits all the fine things that can be said of it.

One of our popular writers and lecturers upon birds told me this incident: He had engaged to take two city girls out for a walk in the country, to teach them the names of the birds they might see and hear. Before they started, he read to them Henry van Dyke's poem on the song sparrow,—one of our best bird-poems,—telling them that the song sparrow was one of the first birds they were likely to hear. As they proceeded with their walk, sure enough, there by the roadside was a sparrow in song. The bird man called the attention of his companions to it. It was some time before the unpracticed ears of the girls could make it out; then one of them said (the poem she had just heard, I suppose, still ringing in her ears), "What! that little squeaky thing?" The sparrow's song meant nothing to her at all, and how could she share the enthusiasm of the poet? Probably the warble of the robin, or the call of the meadowlark or of the highhole, if they chanced to hear them, meant no more to these girls. If we have no associations with these sounds, they will mean very little to us. Their merit as musical performances is very slight. It is as signs of joy and love in nature, as heralds of spring, and as the spirit of the woods and fields made audible, that they appeal to us. The drumming of the woodpeckers and of the ruffed grouse give great pleasure to a countryman, though these sounds have not the quality of real music. It is the same with the call of the migrating geese or the voice of any wild thing: our pleasure in them is entirely apart from any considerations of music. Why does the wild flower, as we chance upon it in the woods or bogs, give us more pleasure than the more elaborate flower of the garden or lawn? Because it comes as a surprise, offers a greater contrast with its surroundings, and suggests a spirit in wild nature that seems to take thought of itself and to aspire to beautiful forms.

The songs of caged birds are always disappointing, because such birds have nothing but their musical qualities to recommend them to us. We have separated them from that which gives quality and, meaning to their songs. One recalls Emerson's lines:—

"I thought the sparrow's note from heaven,
Singing at dawn on the alder bough;
I brought him home, in his nest, at even;
He sings the song, but it cheers not now,
For I did not bring home the river and sky;—
He sang to my ear,—they sang to my eye."

I have never yet seen a caged bird that I wanted,—at least, not on account of its song,—nor a wild flower that I wished to transfer to my garden. A caged skylark will sing its song sitting on a bit of turf in the bottom of the cage; but you want to stop your ears, it is so harsh and sibilant and penetrating. But up there against the morning sky, and above the wide expanse of fields, what delight we have in it! It is not the concord of sweet sounds: it is the soaring spirit of gladness and ecstasy raining down upon us from "heaven's gate."

Then, if to the time and the place one could only add the association, or hear the bird through the vista of the years, the song touched with the magic of youthful memories! One season a friend in England sent me a score of skylarks in a cage. I gave them their liberty in a field near my place. They drifted away, and I never heard them or saw them again. But one Sunday a Scotchman from a neighboring city called upon me, and declared with visible excitement that on his way along the road he had heard a skylark. He was not dreaming; he knew it was a skylark, though he had not heard one since he had left the banks of the Doon, a quarter of a century or more before. What pleasure it gave him! How much more the song meant to him than it would have meant to me! For the moment he was on his native heath again. Then I told him about the larks I had liberated, and he seemed to enjoy it all over again with renewed appreciation.

Many years ago some skylarks were liberated on Long Island, and they became established there, and may now occasionally be heard in certain localities. One summer day a friend of mine was out there observing them; a lark was soaring and singing in the sky above him. An old Irishman came along, and suddenly stopped as if transfixed to the spot; a look of mingled delight and incredulity came into his face. Was he indeed hearing the bird of his youth? He took off his hat, turned his face skyward, and with moving lips and streaming eyes stood a long time regarding the bird. "Ah," my friend thought, "if I could only hear that song with his ears!" How it brought back his youth and all those long-gone days on his native hills!

The power of bird-songs over us is so much a matter of association that every traveler to other countries finds the feathered songsters of less merit than those he left behind. The stranger does not hear the birds in the same receptive, uncritical frame of mind as does the native; they are not in the same way the voices of the place and the season. What music can there be in that long, piercing, far-heard note of the first meadowlark in spring to any but a native, or in the "o-ka-lee" of the red-shouldered starling as he rests upon the willows in March? A stranger would probably recognize melody and a wild woodsy quality in the flutings of the veery thrush; but how much more they would mean to him after he had spent many successive Junes threading our northern trout-streams and encamping on their banks! The veery will come early in the morning, and again at sundown, and perch above your tent, and blow his soft, reverberant note for many minutes at a time. The strain repeats the echoes of the limpid stream in the halls and corridors of the leafy woods.

While in England in 1882, I rushed about two or three counties in late June and early July, bent on hearing the song of the nightingale, but missed it by a few days, and in some cases, as it seemed, only by a few hours. The nightingale seems to be wound up to go only so long, or till about the middle of June, and it is only by a rare chance that you hear one after that date. Then I came home to hear a nightingale in song one winter morning in a friend's house in the city. It was a curious let-down to my enthusiasm. A caged song in a city chamber in broad daylight, in lieu of the wild, free song in the gloaming of an English landscape! I closed my eyes, abstracted myself from my surroundings, and tried my best to fancy myself listening to the strain back there amid the scenes I had haunted about Haslemere and Godalming, but with poor success, I suspect. The nightingale's song, like the lark's, needs vista, needs all the accessories of time and place. The song is not all in the singing, any more than the wit is all in the saying. It is in the occasion, the surroundings, the spirit of which it is the expression. My friend said that the bird did not fully let itself out. Its song was a brilliant medley of notes,— no theme that I could detect,—like the lark's song in this respect; all the notes of the field and forest appeared to be the gift of this bird, but what tone! what accent! like that of a great poet!

Nearly every May I am seized with an impulse to go back to the scenes of my youth, and hear the bobolinks in the home meadows once more. I am sure they sing there better than anywhere else. They probably drink nothing but dew, and the dew distilled in those high pastoral regions has surprising virtues. It gives a clear, full, vibrant quality to the birds' voices that I have never heard elsewhere. The night of my arrival, I leave my southern window open, so that the meadow chorus may come pouring in before I am up in the morning. How it does transport me athwart the years, and make me a boy again, sheltered by the paternal wing! On one occasion, the third morning after my arrival, a bobolink appeared with a new note in his song. The note sounded like the word "baby" uttered with a peculiar, tender resonance: but it was clearly an interpolation; it did not belong there; it had no relation to the rest of the song. Yet the bird never failed to utter it with the same joy and confidence as the rest of his song. Maybe it was the beginning of a variation that will in time result in an entirely new bobolink song.

On my last spring visit to my native hills, my attention was attracted to another songster not seen or heard there in my youth, namely, the prairie horned lark. Flocks of these birds used to be seen in some of the Northern States in the late fall during their southern migrations; but within the last twenty years they have become regular summer residents in the hilly parts of many sections of New York and New England. They are genuine skylarks, and lack only the powers of song to make them as attractive as their famous cousins of Europe.

The larks are ground-birds when they perch, and sky-birds when they sing; from the turf to the clouds—nothing between. Our horned lark mounts upward on quivering wing in the true lark fashion, and, spread out against the sky at an altitude of two or three hundred feet, hovers and sings. The watcher and listener below holds him in his eye, but the ear catches only a faint, broken, half-inarticulate note now and then—mere splinters, as it were, of the song of the skylark. The song of the latter is continuous, and is loud and humming; it is a fountain of jubilant song up there in the sky: but our lark sings in snatches; at each repetition of its notes it dips forward and downward a few feet, and then rises again. One day I kept my eye upon one until it had repeated its song one hundred and three times; then it closed its wings, and dropped toward the earth like a plummet, as does its European congener. While I was watching the bird, a bobolink flew over my head, between me and the lark, and poured out his voluble and copious strain. "What a contrast," I thought, "between the voice of the spluttering, tongue-tied lark, and the free, liquid, and varied song of the bobolink!"

I have heard of a curious fact in the life-histories of these larks in the West. A Michigan woman once wrote me that her brother, who was an engineer on an express train that made daily trips between two Western cities, reported that many birds were struck by the engine every day, and killed— often as many as thirty on a trip of sixty miles. Birds of many kinds were killed, but the most common was a bird that went in flocks, the description of which answered to the horned lark. Since then I have read in a Minnesota newspaper that many horned larks are killed by railroad locomotives in that State. It was thought that the birds sat behind the rails to get out of the wind, and on starting up in front of the advancing train, were struck down by the engine. The Michigan engineer referred to thought that the birds gathered upon the track to earth their wings, or else to pick up the grain that leaks out of the wheat-trains, and sows the track from Dakota to the seaboard. Probably the wind which they might have to face in getting up was the prime cause of their being struck. One does not think of the locomotive as a bird-destroyer, though it is well known that many of the smaller mammals often fall beneath it.

A very interesting feature of our bird-songs is the wing-song, or song of ecstasy. It is not the gift of many of our birds. Indeed, less than a dozen species are known to me as ever singing on the wing. It seems to spring from more intense excitement and self-abandonment than the ordinary song delivered from the perch. When its joy reaches the point of rapture, the bird is literally carried off its feet, and up it goes into the air, pouring out its song as a rocket pours out its sparks. The skylark and the bobolink habitually do this, while a few others of our birds do it only on occasions. One summer, up in the Catskills, I added another name to my list of ecstatic singers—that of the vesper sparrow. Several times I heard a new song in the air, and caught a glimpse of the bird as it dropped back to the earth. My attention would be attracted by a succession of hurried, chirping notes, followed by a brief burst of song, then by the vanishing form of the bird. One day I was lucky enough to see the bird as it was rising to its climax in the air, and to identify it as the vesper sparrow. The burst of song that crowned the upward flight of seventy-five or one hundred feet was brief; but it was brilliant and striking, and entirely unlike the leisurely chant of the bird while upon the ground. It suggested a lark, but was less buzzing or humming. The preliminary chirping notes, uttered faster and faster as the bird mounted in the air, were like the trail of sparks which a rocket emits before its grand burst of color at the top of its flight.

It is interesting to note that this bird is quite lark-like in its color and markings, having the two lateral white quills in the tail, and it has the habit of elevating the feathers on the top of the head so as to suggest a crest. The solitary skylark that I discovered several years ago in a field near me was seen on several occasions paying his addresses to one of these birds, but the vesper-bird was shy, and eluded all his advances.

Probably the perch-songster among our ordinary birds that is most regularly seized with the fit of ecstasy that results in this lyric burst in the air, as I described in my first book, "Wake Robin," over thirty years ago, is the oven-bird, or wood-accentor—the golden-crowned thrush of the old ornithologists. Every loiterer about the woods knows this pretty, speckled-breasted, olive-backed little bird, which walks along over the dry leaves a few yards from him, moving its head as it walks, like a miniature domestic fowl. Most birds are very stiff-necked, like the robin, and as they run or hop upon the ground, carry the head as if it were riveted to the body. Not so the oven-bird, or the other birds that walk, as the cow-bunting, or the quail, or the crow. They move the head forward with the movement of the feet. The sharp, reiterated, almost screeching song of the oven-bird, as it perches on a limb a few feet from the ground, like the words,"preacher, preacher, preacher," or "teacher, teacher, teacher," uttered louder and louder, and repeated six or seven times, is also familiar to most ears; but its wild, ringing, rapturous burst of song in the air high above the tree-tops is not so well known. From a very prosy, tiresome, unmelodious singer, it is suddenly transformed for a brief moment into a lyric poet of great power. It is a great surprise. The bird undergoes a complete transformation. Ordinarily it is a very quiet, demure sort of bird. It walks about over the leaves, moving its head like a little hen; then perches on a limb a few feet from the ground and sends forth its shrill, rather prosy, unmusical chant. Surely it is an ordinary, common-place bird. But wait till the inspiration of its flight-song is upon it. What a change! Up it goes through the branches of the trees, leaping from limb to limb, faster and faster, till it shoots from the tree-tops fifty or more feet into the air above them, and bursts into an ecstasy of song, rapid, ringing, lyrical; no more like its habitual performance than a match is like a rocket; brief but thrilling; emphatic but musical. Having reached its climax of flight and song, the bird closes its wings and drops nearly perpendicularly downward like the skylark. If its song were more prolonged, it would rival the song of that famous bird. The bird does this many times a day during early June, but oftenest at twilight.

The song in quality and general cast is like that of its congener, the water-accentor, which, however, I believe is never delivered on the wing. From its habit of singing at twilight, and from the swift, darting motions of the bird, I am inclined to think that in it we have solved the mystery of Thoreau's "night-warbler," that puzzled and eluded him for years. Emerson told him he must beware of finding and booking it, lest life should have nothing more to show him. The older ornithologists must have heard this song many times, but they never seem to have suspected the identity of the singer.

Other birds that sing on the wing are the meadowlark, goldfinch, purple finch, indigo-bird, Maryland yellow-throat, and woodcock. The flight-song of the woodcock I have heard but twice in my life. The first time was in the evening twilight about the middle of April. The bird was calling in the dusk "yeap, yeap," or "seap, seap," from the ground,—a peculiar reedy call. Then, by and by, it started upward on an easy slant, that peculiar whistling of its wings alone heard; then, at an altitude of one hundred feet or more, it began to float about in wide circles and broke out in an ecstatic chipper, almost a warble at times, with a peculiar smacking musical quality; then, in a minute or so, it dropped back to the ground again, not straight down like the lark, but more spirally, and continued its call as before. In less than five minutes it was up again. The next time, a few years later, I heard the song in company with a friend, Dr. Clara Barrus. Let me give the woman's impression of the song as she afterward wrote it up for a popular journal.

"The sunset light was flooding all this May loveliness of field and farm and distant wood; song sparrows were blithely pouring out happiness by the throatful; peepers were piping and toads trilling, and we thought it no hardship to wait in such a place till the dusk should gather, and the wary woodcock announce his presence. But hark! while yet 'tis light, only a few rods distant, I hear that welcome 'seap ... seap,' and lo! a chipper and a chirr, and past us he flies,—a direct, slanting upward flight, somewhat labored,—his bill showing long against the reddened sky. 'He has something in his mouth,' I start to say, when I bethink me what a long bill he has. Around, above us he flies in wide, ambitious circles, the while we are enveloped, as it were, in that hurried chippering sound—fine, elusive, now near, now distant. How rapid is the flight! Now it sounds faster and faster, 'like a whiplash flashed through the air,' said my friend; up, up he soars, till he becomes lost to sight at the instant that his song ends in that last mad ecstasy that just precedes his alighting."

The meadowlark sings in a level flight, half hovering in the air, giving voice to a rapid medley of lark-like notes. The goldfinch also sings in a level flight, beating the air slowly with its wings broadly open, and pouring out its jubilant, ecstatic strain I think it indulges in this wing-song only in the early season. After the mother bird has begun sitting, the male circles about within earshot of her, in that curious undulating flight, uttering his "per-chic-o-pee, per-chic-o-pee," while the female calls back to him in the tenderest tones, "Yes, lovie; I hear you." The indigo-bird and the purple finch, when their happiness becomes too full and buoyant for them longer to control it, launch into the air, and sing briefly, ecstatically, in a tremulous, hovering flight. The air-song of these birds does not differ essentially from the song delivered from the perch, except that it betrays more excitement, and hence is a more complete lyrical rapture.

The purple finch is our finest songster among the finches. Its strain is so soft and melodious, and touched with such a childlike gayety and plaintiveness, that I think it might sound well even in a cage inside a room, if the bird would only sing with the same joyous abandonment, which, of course, it would not do.

It is not generally known that individual birds of the same species show different degrees of musical ability. This is often noticed in caged birds, among which the principle of variation seems more active; but an attentive observer notes the same fact in wild birds. Occasionally he hears one that in powers of song surpasses all its fellows. I have heard a sparrow, an oriole, and a wood thrush, each of which had a song of its own that far exceeded any other. I stood one day by a trout-stream, and suspended my fishing for several minutes to watch a song sparrow that was singing on a dry limb before me. He had five distinct songs, each as markedly different from the others as any human songs, which he repeated one after the other. He may have had a sixth or a seventh, but he bethought himself of some business in the next field, and flew away before he had exhausted his repertory. I once had a letter from Robert Louis Stevenson, who said he had read an account I had written of the song of the English blackbird. He said I might as well talk of the song of man; that every blackbird had its own song; and then he told me of a remarkable singer he used to hear somewhere amid the Scottish hills. But his singer was, of course, an exception; twenty-four blackbirds out of every twenty-five probably sing the same song, with no appreciable variations: but the twenty-fifth may show extraordinary powers. I told Stevenson that his famous singer had probably been to school to some nightingale on the

Continent or in southern England. I might have told him of the robin I once heard here that sang with great spirit and accuracy the song of the brown thrasher, or of another that had the note of the whip-poor-will interpolated in the regular robin song, or of still another that had the call of the quail. In each case the bird had probably heard the song and learned it while very young. In the Trossachs, in Scotland, I followed a song thrush about for a long time, attracted by its peculiar song. It repeated over and over again three or four notes of a well-known air, which it might have caught from some shepherd boy whistling to his flock or to his cow.

The songless birds — why has Nature denied them this gift? But they nearly all have some musical call or impulse that serves them very well. The quail has his whistle, the woodpecker his drum, the pewee his plaintive cry, the chickadee his exquisitely sweet call, the highhole his long, repeated "wick, wick, wick," one of the most welcome sounds of spring, the jay his musical gurgle, the hawk his scream, the crow his sturdy caw. Only one of our pretty birds of the orchard is reduced to an all but inaudible note, and that is the cedar-bird.